Divine Intervention

*A Mother's Story
of Hope and Healing*

Christina Andre'

Copyright © 2020 by Christina Andre'

All Rights Reserved

Published by Hodge Publishing
17165 Linda Lane
Conroe, Texas 77306

Scriptures taken from the Holy Bible, New International Version®, NIV®. Copyright © 1973, 1978, 1984, 2011 by Biblica, Inc.™ Used by permission of Zondervan. All rights reserved worldwide. www.zondervan.com The "NIV" and "New International Version" are trademarks registered in the United States Patent and Trademark Office by Biblica, Inc.®

No part of this e-book may be reproduced, stored, or transmitted in any form or by any means including mechanical or electronic without prior written permission from the author.

ISBN 978-0-578-68863-3

1. Christianity
2. Memoirs
3. Family

Dedication

To my daughters, Madison and Ava

Considering the time I've spent carrying each of you, you have also carried me in many ways. You've given me unconditional love in abundance and I thank God for allowing me to spend this life as your mom. My prayer for you both is that you always know when your heart breaks, God will heal you. When you lose your way, God will guide you. When you feel there is nothing left, dig deeper. Seek Him always. Lastly, there is nothing either of you will ever do that could outweigh my love for you. You are the greatest loves of my life.

You is kind. You is smart. You is important.

Description

I used to believe in God similar to the way my daughters believed in the tooth fairy. My faith was shaky and questionable at best. A series of events in my life caused great heartache for me from a young age, which made me question God's mercy and whether He even loved me. As I stood at the proverbial crossroad of hurt and hopelessness, God intervened and saved me from a self-destructive path. His divine intervention in my life has instilled in me a desire to share God's love with others. This book is my walk with God—my journey from brokenness to a discovery of faith, my experiences, and my sharing the goodness that has been bestowed upon a once very broken soul. I don't believe in God anymore—I know Him, I trust Him, and I seek Him day after day.

CONTENTS

Introduction 1

A Damaged Daughter 3

Where Healing Begins 6

Adam and Eve 9

Our Intercessor 12

The Bleeding Woman 14

Who Is God? 17

Lies and Deception 20

The Spirit of Sonship 23

Home Team 26

I've Been Set Free 29

Anchored in the Storm 32

The Cure 40

Advancing God's Kingdom 42

The Chosen One 45

The Lesson of Humility 47

My Roots 50

The Upper Room 54

The Purest Love of All 58

Defining Moments 63

You're Invited! 66

Introduction

— John 1:1-5

In the beginning was the Word, and the Word was with God, and the Word was God. He was with God in the beginning. Through him all things were made; without him nothing was made that has been made. In him was life, and that life was the light of all mankind. The light shines in the darkness, and the darkness has not overcome it.

Growing up in South Louisiana, it was common to see everyone and their grandmas in church on Sundays.

The old wooden pews of St. Bridget Catholic Church were where we took our best naps. Those same pews were where we got the "Zip your lips, or else…" look from my Gamzy and Pops when we were being antsy during service. Stand up, sit down, kneel, repeat. I remember the smell of the church and the blast of cold air as the doors opened.

Sunday mornings before church were the best. There were always a few of us either fighting to stand on the toilet as Gamzy applied her lipstick or sitting in Pops' recliner drinking coffee milk while waiting for the "In a Minute" cartoon commercial to flash across the television screen. Like most children, going to church always seemed more like a chore to me. But later my grandparents passed away, pieces of my family separated over time, and everything changed.

Decades passed before I attended a play called "The God Box" based on a book written by a Christian woman named Mary Lou Quinlan. This play is a story of her mom who had passed away. Somewhere along the way, Quinlan discovered multiple boxes filled with little notes to God handwritten by her mom. Simple prayers for people whom her mom had encountered throughout the years. She had a praying momma and those prayer-filled boxes meant everything to Quinlan.

I remember sitting there thinking, "I want to do this for my girls." From that day forward, I have carried my God Book in hand to every church service and Bible study. When my girls are older, I want them to have a bin filled with my God Books, where they will be able to read everything I've learned throughout my walk with God, what certain scriptures mean to me, and how or when certain people and experiences affected my life and theirs.

I've spent a lot of time staring at an old Bible. Sadly, I realize and regret how much I previously missed out on. Before moving any further into this, I only ask that you hear my heart when I say these words are a collection of my own personal beliefs. If your beliefs differ (sometimes they will), that's okay. One of my favorite pastors said a mouthful when he said, "I don't have a dog in anyone's fight. I just want to know the *truth*."

A Damaged Daughter

— Jeremiah 1:5

Before I formed you in the womb I knew you, and before you were born I consecrated you; I appointed you a prophet to the nations.

Although we all have access to the same book, our interpretations of scripture may differ. Similarly, our interpretations of religious traditions and practices vary too. In my opinion, Christianity shouldn't be about rituals and rules. Christianity is about relationships and especially a relationship with God. The Bible is filled with stories about people who have sinned, and a good, loving Father.

It's disheartening to think of how many years I spent believing that I had to do certain things and pray a specific way to be close to God. To be quite honest, it was exhausting! That same exhaustion, along with my inability to cope with the aftermath of childhood trauma, played a significant role in my drifting away from Catholicism. It certainly wasn't that I found a "better" religion. I was empty handed.

I felt as if the church focused so much time on teaching how to prevent from going to Hell rather than teaching the way to Heaven. I could figure out the path to hell on my own—I had perfected the art of bad decision making and I was good at it! I thought the righteousness of God was a standard by which we would all be judged rather than something He freely gives to us. Of all the years I spent attending Catechism and observing Holy Days of Obligation, I walked away feeling unaccepted and empty. I had come to a point in life where I was tired of trying to reach an unreachable God.

No longer did I want to attend mass out of guilt-ridden obligation to serve a God that I didn't know. I couldn't understand how God could love me and have me endure years of sexual abuse as a child.

How could He leave me to witness my mother suffer physical, verbal, and emotional abuse? And why? God could have picked one struggle but why both at the same time?

I dropped church like a bad habit, only to pick up a few bad habits of my own. I didn't think about God as much anymore. I was 15 years old when I witnessed a drug overdose. My jaw tightens when I go back to that night because I will never forget the way her body slouched down on the balcony and my being so disconnected from reality that I continued to party the night away.

By the time I celebrated my 16th birthday, I had poisoned my body with ecstasy, acid, angel dust, peyote (mescaline), ketamine, cocaine, and crystal methamphetamine, among other things. My days were filled with one of two emotions: sober and damaged beyond repair or high and on top of the world. The teenager in me thought I had found the answer to my problems—Stay high!

Boy, was I wrong.

The real problems arrived when that drug-induced euphoria faded for good and I was still alive and extremely broken. Somedays I was depressed, other days I was anxious and at times I felt both. I wish I would have been open to talking to my parents about the things I was struggling with, but I was stubborn and prideful.

I've prayed long and hard about whether I should include this part of my story in my book. In fact, many tears fell as I wrote this piece. At the time, I was a teenager. My daughters are now teenagers and I also share my life with three boys whom I love like they are my own children, two of which are teenagers. I don't want my kids to read this and think it's cool or think it can't be so bad since I turned out the way I did. I don't want my parents hurt by reading this or to feel like they failed me. My mother, my father, my step-mother, and my step-father are all phenomenal people and at times were the only sense of normalcy that I had. My step-mother always told me kids don't come with instructions and this is true. I'm sure they all wished for a step-by-step manual to deal with me in my teenage years.

Where Healing Begins

— Jeremiah 1:5

Before I formed you in the womb I knew you, and before you were born I consecrated you; I appointed you a prophet to the nations.

I birthed my oldest daughter at 20 years old in July 2004 and my youngest was born in March 2006. God entrusted me to grow two small humans whom I would later learn were terrifyingly just like their mother! From that moment on, I knew my life was no longer my own and I was living for something larger than myself. It was my job to break the cycle of dysfunction, abuse, and addiction for my girls and I was determined to do just that—come hell or high water.

Their father and I never married. We separated when my youngest daughter was a few months old.

There I was, a baby with two babies. No job, no vehicle, and no clue, but I did have bills and two babies to feed. It was only a matter of time before I planted my feet firmly in a job that gave me the resources I needed to be both a single mother and a dedicated employee. If my girls were sick, they were allowed to come to work with me. Those next few years were tough as I had to find a good balance in life for myself and my girls, but we kept moving forward.

Looking back, I can clearly see the hand of God directing my path and divinely placing certain people in our lives at certain times. A few of those special people would lead us to a small non-denominational church in New Iberia, LA. Coming from a Catholic family, this was a new experience for me. A breath of fresh air, in my opinion. There were no rules or rituals; it was come as you are. I spent the first few services in awe, looking around at the varying colors of people from all different walks of life. Some were married, some single, some recovering addicts who were broken and suffering.

There I was, a deer in the headlights, not sure what to make of it all. We all shared one thing in common: we were hungry for the word of God. For the first time in my life, I felt a sense of belonging.

I listened to the Pastor speak of his own sinfulness and how God delivered him from addiction decades before. I recall sitting in that pew in disbelief of what he said. He finished that sermon with a recipe to fight addiction: "Change your playgrounds, your playmates, and your play things." Those words are handwritten in one of my first God Books and that Pastor is forever etched in my heart.

That church became my safe place to fall every Sunday and sometimes on Wednesday afternoons as well. It was my home and those people became my spiritual family. This is where I acknowledged Christ as my Savior and began my walk with God.

There have been many Christians whom I have drawn close to along the way. Each of them has planted seeds in me and for that I am so thankful. I will never forget the response of my small group leader when I asked about her beliefs. Very simply, she said, "I believe in this book," as she raised her Bible. She proceeded with, "And I believe a dude came down to earth and died for the sins of mankind." (Yes, she used the word dude!) I was so taken aback by her response, then I thought to myself, *That's my people!* as my dad would say.

Adam and Eve

— Matthew 7:9-11

Which of you, if your son asks for bread, will give him a stone? Or if he asks for a fish, will give him a snake? If you, then, though you are evil, know how to give good gifts to your children, how much more will your Father in heaven give good gifts to those who ask him!

Genesis 1:31 says, "God saw all that He had made, and it was very good..." God spoke everything into existence except mankind. He said, "Let there be light," and there was light. He said, "Let there be a vault between the waters..." and He called it the sky. And so, it continued, until He said, "Let us *make* mankind in our image..." Unlike everything else, He lovingly handcrafted us in his image and likeness.

Basically, we are like his fingerprints! Genesis 2:7 says that He breathed into us the "breath of life."

The story of Adam and Eve is a clear example of God's love for us, His children. Neither Adam nor Eve were ashamed of being naked until they ate from the tree of knowledge of good and evil after God had commanded them not to do so. Only then did they hide out of shame. Genesis 3:9 says, "But the Lord God called to the man, 'where are you?'" Reading this verse was my "Aha!" moment. He looks for us!

Both Adam and Eve were banished from the Garden of Eden as a consequence of their actions, and they were not allowed to eat from the tree of life. They had forfeited their shot at eternal life. One might think this was done in mercy because granting them eternal life at this point would mean they would spend eternity hiding from God because of their sin. I've certainly hidden from God more times than I'd like to admit. How foolish of me to think He doesn't already know me. He made me! A dear friend of mine once told me, "God sees everything from end to beginning." That is powerful!

God walked this same earth in human form and experienced temptations and suffering, so that He could relate to us. I imagine He'd say, "Been there, done that, already have the T-shirt." Truly, the only thing that set His humanity apart from ours is that He was free of sin. Jesus was the true character of God in human form. You see, it's not until we learn God's character that we can appreciate His love for us. He is the Good Shepherd and we are His sheep.

I never realized how lost I was until He found me. Let me be clear when I say that He found *me*. I did not find Him; God wasn't the lost one, Christina was. I lived 30 years believing I was just a skeleton in a skin suit, afraid of life, death, and everything in between. Suddenly, I realized that somehow I'd been transformed. I'd been pursued by God. I had been pursued by *God!* Who am I that the highest king would welcome *me?* This was a life-changing revelation.

All too often, we forget the truth about sin. There are no lesser sins. We all fall short of the glory of God; we live in a fallen world. I don't deserve salvation—in fact, none of us do. The good news is that God's mercy is brand new Every. Single. Day! The Bible says that we have been saved by grace through faith. Our Father has delightfully given us a true gift; His delight is like the feeling you get when you give your child a gift. How awful it would feel if your child refused a gift that you poured your heart into giving.

Our Intercessor

— John 3:5-6

Very truly I tell you, no one can enter the kingdom of God unless they are born of water and the Spirit. Flesh gives birth to flesh, but the Spirit gives birth to spirit.

I had always wondered what it meant when someone spoke of the time in their life when they received the gift of the Holy Spirit or when they referred to the moment they grew in their faith. When questioned about it, the response was always the same: "you just know,"—which reminds me of when someone asks what something tastes like and the reply is that it tastes like chicken. Really? Is that the default response to everything? I would later learn there was a lot of truth in the "you just know" answer.

I'm not able to pinpoint the exact date and time that I grew in my faith, but I can tell you that it happened over time. And then one day I woke up and I *undeniably knew*! I had received the gift of revelation without even realizing it. Suddenly, everything made perfect sense. I had learned what those tugs on my heartstrings meant and how to acknowledge and abide by them.

It took me more than thirty years to hear the voice of God, but He does indeed speak to me and now I listen. If I had to guess, my Gamzy is probably shaking her head, saying, "Tete dure, she finally gets it." My heart aches when I think about the people who spend their whole lives never knowing what this feels like. I remember the times in the past when I'd have rather eaten broken glass than sit and listen to "holy rollers" tell me how great our God is. All these years later, I'm the holy roller and I have no apologies for those who'd rather eat broken glass. Most days, I wish I had a mountain to stand on to be able to tell the world about our Father and His Son, our Savior. I'd loudly proclaim for all to hear that His Spirit dwells in the heart of believers and a real-life transformation occurs when you are born again.

The Bleeding Woman

— **Mark 2:17**

It is not the healthy who need a doctor, but the sick. I have not come to call the righteous, but sinners.

I remember the first story that came to life for me in the Bible and how excited I was to tell anyone who would listen about it. A woman had suffered for 12 years with a condition that caused her to bleed constantly. The Bible doesn't specify her condition, but it's clear she had exhausted every resource she had in her attempts to get well again.

Not only was she consumed with this terrible condition, but I think it's safe to say that she spent most of those years with little to no social contact. In early Jewish culture, women were considered second-class citizens, at best. Men wouldn't touch a menstruating woman, whether her bleeding was natural or caused by disease, lest they become "ceremonially unclean."

You can imagine how this woman must have been treated. They probably avoided her like the plague! Mark 5:27 says, "When she heard about Jesus, she came up behind him in the crowd and touched his cloak." According to the Bible, she thought, "If I can only touch the hem of his garment, I will be made well." Although the crowd had made it nearly impossible to get close to Jesus, she reached him and the instant she touched His clothing, the bleeding stopped. What a difference there is between the crowds who are just curious about Jesus and those who reach out and touch Him.

My favorite part of the story is when Jesus turns around and asks, "Who touched me?" Really? He's Jesus; He knew who touched him! But I believe Jesus asked that question for two very important reasons. First, He wanted to show the woman that his cloak had no magical powers and hadn't healed her. It was her faith that healed her. Faith, and faith alone, releases God's healing power. Second, and most importantly, Jesus took that opportunity to teach the woman and the crowd that there is no one too dirty or unclean for God. His strength is made perfect in our weakness.

Jesus came to give us life and make us completely new. He bridged the gap between God and man by paying the price for our sins. We shouldn't let the shame prevent us from building a relationship with Him. When I think about this, my comical mind takes over and I visualize Jesus walking among us somewhere in Louisiana. Here He will likely find a Boudreaux or a Thibodaux, maybe even a Broussard or two, who want to feed him gumbo or share fishing stories.

"Hey Jesus, thanks for hanging on that cross for us, but no thanks, we're clean already. False alarm!" Followed by a fist bump. Can you picture His surprised reaction? "I did all of that, and they didn't even need to be saved?" Surely, you catch my drift and understand where I'm going with this. The fact that we are unclean is the very reason we should touch Him. God took our sins and placed them on Jesus when He died on the cross. He took the righteousness of Jesus and placed it on us.

Who Is God?

— John 17:3

Now this is eternal life: that they know you, the only true God, and Jesus Christ, whom you have sent.

My interest is piqued when I consider other religions and worldly views outside of Christianity. I think it's fair to say most people have little interest in the details or religious beliefs outside of what they believe to be true. It was my spiritual quest for truth that piqued such interest. I've found that even major Non-Christian religions give an account of Jesus. He's described as a prophet, a healer, a miracle worker and a holy man. He's the common denominator.

That alone should cause everyone to stop and take a good look into who Jesus really is.

Personally, I've had discussions with non-believers, some of whom are family to me. In my experience, the same questions always arise, namely why do you believe in someone you've never met and someone you can't see? You can't even visit a grave, they say. Please, listen closely…meeting God will never be the same as meeting your next-door neighbor because He's *not* your next-door neighbor. No, I've never stood before the physical Jesus before, but I've been in His presence many times, and He has met me in my mess every time I've needed Him. Have I seen Him? Sure, I have! I've seen Him in the hearts and actions of believers.

My very first small group through church was a Freedom Group. Freedom is a 12-week course focused on certain areas of spiritual growth such as living in the tree of life, walking in the spirit, learning to speak words of life, and becoming a vessel God can use, etc. At the end of those 12 weeks is a powerful 2-day Freedom Conference. To be part of a Freedom group and experience a Freedom Conference is something I hope for everyone. When I signed up for my first Freedom group, I remember thinking "I don't need this but what the heck, it can't hurt." I didn't realize just how bad I needed that.

God spoke to me in my first Freedom Conference. As prayer time neared, prayer partners lined the walls of the sanctuary. I recall sitting in the pew with my head down as my row was awaiting its turn to be assigned a prayer partner.

I prayed to God, "Okay, where are you? Show me!" I can't say exactly what I was expecting to see, but something came over me and I heard, "Look around. I'm everywhere." As I lifted my head, I saw the entire sanctuary lined with prayer. I saw women praying with women and men praying with men. I heard heartfelt cries as I watched the weight of heavy burdens fall to the floor just as easy as tears were shed.

My face felt flushed, and as I smiled to hide my cry, I thought to myself, "This is it! This is what the heart of God looks like!" Paul says in the book of Romans that you don't need any more evidence that God exists—look up and look around!

Lastly, there's a very important reason why Christians can't visit their Savior's grave. This very reason is the foundation on which all of Christianity stands. The grave is empty! He has defeated death!

Lies and Deception

— James 4:7

Submit yourselves, then, to God. Resist the devil, and he will flee from you.

The Bible says that we can only serve one master. We either belong to God or we belong to the enemy. Are you straddling the fence, or have you chosen a side?

Many of us visualize the devil as a little red man with a pitchfork and a pointy tail, or as a nightmarishly ugly creature. This is how he tries to deceive us. He's such a liar! Many people believe that Lucifer was the angel of worship, as well as the most beautiful, powerful, and intelligent angel of all. But he wasn't content to worship and serve his Creator; instead his pride led him to believe that he was better than God. He began to fight God which resulted in his fall to earth and his name being changed from Lucifer, meaning "morning star," to Satan, which means "adversary."

Revelation 12 describes Satan as an enormous red dragon whose tail "hurled" one-third of the stars in the sky to earth. According to Hebrew tradition, one-third of all the angels in Heaven fell with Satan.

I believe the stars hurled to earth by the red dragon in Revelation 12 signify those fallen angels. Now, do you think Satan works alone?

While the Bible doesn't give us the exact number of angels in Heaven, Scripture uses terms such as "innumerable", "myriads", and "thousands upon thousands." Lucifer happened to be one of only three angels identified in the Bible by name. Michael was the fighter, Gabriel was the messenger, and I believe Lucifer was the worshipper. We know that angels have free will and Lucifer made a choice. After his fall from God's grace, God still had His fighter and His messenger, but He was missing a key player: His worshipper.

The Bible says God created us for his glory, which is defined as great praise or appreciation that is typically offered in worship. You see, Satan doesn't work against us because of who we are. He works against us because we took his place. He will never again worship before God in the throne room of heaven, but we will!

If Satan can't steal your salvation, he will try his best to steal your joy. Ezekiel 28 mentions the fall of Satan just as clearly as Isaiah 14, but there's something about Isaiah 14:16-17 that makes me chuckle. In short, it says that we are going to look at Satan in the end, partly incredulous and partly bemused, and say, "That's him? Is this 'who shook the earth and made kingdoms tremble?'" I imagine our reaction will be like that of a parent whose child has been bullied at school. Upon seeing the bully, who is probably the smallest in the class, the parent's surprised reaction is: "That's him? This is the one who's been taunting you?"

The enemy truly comes to steal, kill, and destroy. He uses pain and pleasure to make us blind, stupid, and miserable. I spent most of my adult life serving the devil without recognizing it. Before my eyes were opened to the truth, I thought that that's all there was to life. The enemy was working harder at trying to destroy me than I was working to prevent being destroyed. I know who he is now. He's such a liar.

The Spirit of Sonship

— John 1:9-13

The true light that gives light to everyone was coming into the world. He was in the world, and though the world was made through him, the world did not recognize him. He came to that which was his own, but his own did not receive him. Yet to all who did receive him, to those who believed in his name, he gave the right to become children of God—children born not of natural descent, nor of human decision or a husband's will, but born of God.

Romans 8:14 states, "For those who are led by the Spirit of God are the children of God." The passage goes on to say that as the children of God we have not received the spirit of slavery so that we live in fear. Rather, we've received the spirit of adoption or "sonship." The apostle Paul, who wrote the Book of Romans, uses adoption or "sonship" to illustrate the believer's new relationship with God. When a person becomes a Christian, he or she gains all the privileges and responsibilities of a legitimate child in God's family.

In ancient Roman culture, biological parents had the option of disowning their child(ren) for a variety of reasons. As a result, adoption was very meaningful because if someone chose to adopt, it meant that they desired and freely chose the child. Additionally, adoptive parents weren't allowed to disown an adopted child, so this child truly received a new and permanent identity as an heir to their father.

But the adoption process at that time was just that—a process! First, a symbolic sale had to be carried out three times. The biological father would symbolically sell his son and both times he would symbolically buy his son back. The third time he would, again, symbolically sell his son, but he would not buy him back. Finally, the father who wished to adopt would stand before the Roman magistrate and present a legal case for the transference of the person being adopted.

Obviously, you and I don't live under Roman law, but just as the father who wanted to adopt stood before the Roman magistrate, Jesus stood before God the Father to plead our case when he died on the cross. And just as the adoptive parents freely chose and wanted the child they adopted, God fully chooses and desires us!

The adoption process in Roman law took place before seven witnesses. Romans 8:16 says, "The Spirit himself bears witness with our spirit that we are God's children." In the end, the old life of the adopted person is wiped out completely in order that he or she become an heir to the new father's estate.

Initially, this illustration was confusing to me because there's no mention of a daughter when referring to the adoption process. Thank goodness for Google! In my research, I discovered that adoption was a way for Romans to pass down their family fortune and guarantee succession when unable to produce a male heir. It was rare that a daughter would be adopted since women had severely restricted rights.

We may not always feel as though we belong to God, but His inward presence reminds us of who we are, and He encourages us with His love.

Home Team

— 1 Corinthians 13:4-7

Love is patient, love is kind. It does not envy, it does not boast, it is not proud. It does not dishonor others, it is not self-seeking, it is not easily angered, it keeps no record of wrongs. Love does not delight in evil but rejoices with the truth. It always protects, always trusts, always hopes, always perseveres.

The Bible says that the presence of God will drive the pleasure of sin out of your life. I've lost many friends along the way, but if hindsight is 20/20 then I can say with much certainty that I haven't left anyone or anything behind that would be considered a loss at all.

We spend most of our lives lost, calling ourselves depressed while Jesus calls us whole. We attach labels to ourselves, and this becomes our way of thinking.

Many years ago, I had a conversation with my older brother who was going through a rough time in his life. He had no desire to change but plenty of time to feel sorry for himself. I knew better. After all, we don't share the same blood for the fun of it. I don't remember what I asked him, but I will never forget his response. He said, "I've had a rough life, Lu. I'm not strong like you are. I can't shake this."

My first thought was: "We grew up in the same home; I dealt with the same struggles." And there he was, thinking I had somehow made out better than he had. There I stood, just as tired and broken as he was. Although we're different, he and I had always managed to stick together. Sure, I had wised up sooner than he, but there had also been a time when I had to be honest with myself in acknowledging that the majority of those years weren't really "wising up" but rather just being good at covering up my dirt. It was easier to focus on his mess than it was to focus on mine.

I spent years on end praying for God to show up in a big way for him, my niece, and my nephews. Shamefully, I found myself envious, and sometimes even bitter, when God began to move for them. For the life of me, I can't make sense of how or why I thought I deserved what he had more than he did. I'm thankful that God has paid close attention to that piece of my heart in order to bring those feelings to light, and I'm thankful that my niece and nephews have their dad back. His resilience in the face of adversity is worth more than its weight in gold. I'm forever thankful for his wife, the one who stepped up and refuses to step down or give up despite difficulty. If someone were to sit my grandma down and ask her about that woman, she would most likely cry just before she went on about what a true blessing she has been to our family. I do not hesitate to say that I look up to her in more ways than I can count.

I once read an article written by Shauna Niequist. In it she explains:

"Everyone has a home team: It's the people you call when you get a flat tire or when something terrible happens. It's the people who, near or far, know everything that's wrong with you and love you anyways. These are the ones who tell you their secrets, who get themselves a glass of water without asking when they're at your house. These are the people who cry when you cry. These are your people, your middle-of-the-night, no-matter-what people."

Whether near or far, no matter the differences that come, my siblings are the foundation of my home team. I feel blessed beyond measure to know my home team not only consists of an earthly family, but my spiritual family as well. Love always wins!

I've Been Set Free

— John 8:34-36

Very truly I tell you, everyone who sins is a slave to sin. Now a slave has no permanent place in the family, but a son belongs to it forever. So if the Son sets you free, you will be free indeed.

When Abraham Lincoln issued the Emancipation Proclamation, it was a declaration to end slavery. But while it freed all slaves, most stayed with their master because that's all they knew. When I think of how profound this is, the visual image of a caged bird comes to mind. After being caged for so long, the bird may be too afraid to fly once the cage is opened.

This applies to anyone who is a slave to sin, whether we realize this or not. Maybe the addict is afraid to live sober because that means facing life and feeling things without a crutch. What about the women and men who stay in abusive relationships because they are afraid of the unknown? It seems so cliché, but all it takes is just one small leap of faith.

Some of the best decisions I've ever made were those that I carried out with shaky knees, teary eyes, and the crippling reality that if for some reason I fell flat on my face, my two girls were falling with me.

This is where the faith part comes into play, I suppose. In 2009, I added a simple quote to my Facebook profile: "Life is made of small moments. When we begin to change those moments, we begin to change our lives." I couldn't tell you when I got this quote or what it originally meant to me. What I can tell you is that my life has been changed, and I do believe that change was a direct result of many small moments.

There is true freedom in being made new in Christ. I've gained so much throughout this walk thus far, but my list of losses does continue to grow. In fact, I've lost anger, resentment, blame, and hurt, to name a few. I once sat in a pew staring at my pastor as he imparted a powerful message about forgiveness. I thought to myself, *What does forgiveness feel like?* Such a good question, right? I had wondered how I would know if I had truly forgiven someone.

In that exact moment, my pastor looked directly at me and said, "Forgiveness is not a feeling; it's a choice. It's a choice that you will have to make every single day."

I hadn't asked my question out loud, so there's no way he knew to say that right then, but I know that God heard me and answered my question through the pastor. Freedom is a lot like forgiveness in that sense. It's a choice that you have to make every single day. For example,

I choose to be free from anger. I choose to see the good in people. I choose to see the good in myself.

When Jesus shed His blood for us, He washed away our sins. In a court of law, they would say, "Not guilty! Let her go free!" Now I ask, what would those words mean to you if you were on death row?

Anchored in the Storm

— **Psalm 30:11-12**

You turned my wailing into dancing; you removed my sackcloth and clothed me with joy, that my heart may sing your praises and not be silent. Lord my God, I will praise you forever.

No matter where we are in our walk with Christ, it's easiest to have faith and praise God when we are on top of the mountain and life is going as expected. How we respond when we face opposition is what reveals our true faith, or lack thereof. There's no question that we serve a mighty God and that He truly is the Lord of the valleys.

He meets us as we are, where we are, and in ways that we can understand.

The book of Job is personally a tough one for me. It reminds me of a painful season in my life. I've always been the kind to resist change whether that be a change of career, a change in routine, or a change in relationship.

At the time, the combination of changes taking place in my job and my fear of losing one of the most meaningful relationships of my life is what sparked a plethora of uncertainty in me, launching me into an emotional cesspool of depression and anxiety-stricken panic. Even then, I knew there was more behind my pain than what I was facing at the time. Old wounds were resurfacing. There was a hurt little girl inside of me, and she was fighting her way out. It was as if every hurt I had ever experienced in my life flowed out of me all at once.

As I piece together my thoughts in order to tell this part of my story, I find it difficult to do so without shedding a few tears. How I wish I had an ounce of Job's faith during that time.

The Bible describes Job as being a man of God. He was faithful and blessed. It goes on to explain that Satan came before the Lord, and God asked him from where he'd come. Satan responded, "From roaming throughout the earth, going back and forth on it," which reminds me of Peter's warning in 1 Peter 5:8: "Be alert and of sober mind. Your enemy the devil prowls around like a roaring lion looking for someone to devour." God then said to Satan, "Have you considered my servant Job?"

Wait. What? Like most, my immediate reaction to this was to question why God would set Job up like that.

But God knew Job's heart, and He knew Job was good and loyal. He was about to teach old Satan a lesson!

Satan declared to God that Job is only faithful because God had continued to bless him. He argued that if Job were to lose his blessings, he would surely curse God. As the story continues, we discover that Job loses everything, including his family. The Bible points out that

Job's wife was spared, but her presence just caused more suffering for Job because he had to watch her suffer all that they had lost, and he felt her sorrow deeply. The beauty in this story is that Job never lost his faith. He praised God despite his suffering. Job's friends insisted that he must have sinned, and this was God's punishment.

Another friend suggested that God was using this pain to purify Job. While Job remained faithful, his pain and anguish began to overwhelm him. Doubt crept in and he started questioning the value of living a blameless life. He straddled a fine line that could have easily insinuated that God didn't care about him. When God finally spoke, he didn't offer Job any answers. What he did offer Job was peace in the knowledge that sometimes it's better to know God than to know answers.

All too often we think good things are supposed to happen to good people, and bad things are supposed to happen to bad people. It couldn't be farther from the truth to think that we should never face hard times because we are followers of Christ. God never promised that no weapon would be forged against us, although He did promise that those weapons would never prevail. (Isaiah 54:17)

Sometimes suffering can shape us in a way that allows us to walk more confidently in the purpose that God has for our lives.

I've spent as much time trying to forget the painful pieces of myself as I have spent trying to make sense of all the pain. Am I glad it's over? Absolutely.

Would I choose to walk through that difficult period in my life again? Never in a million lifetimes! Do I think God used that experience to do an amazing work in me? I've never been more certain of anything in my life!

Looking forward, I know that I'll experience that measure of heartache again. Life is too unpredictable to think otherwise. The thought of that saddens the deepest parts of me. Having said that, I can say with certainty that I am equipped with a faith that I lacked the first time around. I am not the same person who walked into that storm years ago.

For many years, prior to this challenging time in my life, my prayers focused on two things. First, I prayed that if I was standing in my own way that God would move me. Second, I prayed that God would take from me whatever was not meant for me at the time. Those prayers had so much heart behind them, but I now know that they were both faithless requests.

Not only did I not understand God's character, I didn't know God at all. I didn't know His Son, and I certainly wasn't prepared to receive what I had been asking of Him. Time and time again, I unknowingly treated God as if He was a family heirloom that had been handed down to me from my grandparents. I thought I could stick God in my purse and ask Him to perform magic tricks for me whenever my life didn't look like I thought it should. I'd say an Our Father and a few Hail Marys here or there, and surely God would do exactly as I wanted, right?

Early morning drives to work are one of my favorite times to worship. This special time helps prepare me for my day.

One morning, I listened to the song "Oceans (Where Feet May Fail)" by Hillsong UNITED. As the song played, I visualized Peter stepping out of the boat and walking on water toward Jesus. I was a bit taken aback because I had listened to this song thousand times before and had never previously associated the song with that biblical story before.

Later that day I posted the song on my Facebook wall with a short story of what I had experienced earlier that morning. My post explained that Peter began to sink and became fearful of the storm when he took his eyes off Jesus. At the end of the post I posed a question that at the time seemed insignificant but turned out to be very important to me.

I asked: "How many times do you find yourself sinking because you are too afraid of the storm?" This was the first time in my life that I knew God was speaking to me. It wasn't until a few months later that I would figure out why. He was about to move me, and life as I knew it was about to get messy.

The saying "be careful what you wish for" carries a lot of weight. Countless times I prayed for God to move me, and then when he finally did, I panicked. Nights on end, I prayed that he would take from me anyone or anything that wasn't meant for me.

And then He did.

My entire world seemed to unravel, and I felt so helpless. I found myself in what I can best describe as a game of tug of war with God. It was as if He was saying, *"Okay, Christina. I need this,"* while removing those things from my grasp. I would try to hold on to them while crying, "No. NO. That's not what I meant when I asked you to do that. I need this!"

I can envision His response: *"Ahh, so, you want your daily bread, but you want to tell me how to prepare it?"* I've found myself down many lonely roads in my life but this one—God bless. I could not see the light at the end of the tunnel, although I tried.

At the time, one of my closest friends happened to be going through a tough time as well. She spent many nights with me, just for comfort. As time went on her situation got better, and she went home, but I was still hurting. A few months later, another friend of mine found herself in a difficult period in her life, and, like the last, she spent many nights with me, laughing, but mostly crying. Eventually she overcame her challenges, and she also left me to return home.

There's no need to tell you how the next part of the story goes. I thought to myself that this was old news to everyone but me, and I wondered why it hurt so much. I felt as though I was paying for the long list of terrible things I had done in the past. Life seemed unbearable. I can't count the nights I laid across my bed with my arms wide open, staring at the ceiling and pleading in my loudest voice, "Help me!" or the countless nights I climbed in bed with one of my girls so I didn't feel so alone. There's something deep inside of me that still trembles as I relive that.

Sadly, I didn't have Job-like faith. I prayed, I pleaded, I begged, and I bargained with God to deliver me. In my desperate attempt to regain myself, I sought the advice of a counselor, and I considered a temporary leave of absence from work. Shortly before, I had been demoted from a full-time position to part-time due to my excessive absences and inability to lead my team.

Disconnection notices poured in from every direction. There I was, lying in bed and numb, trying to make sense of the pain. That's the thing about pain—it demands to be felt. There's no going around it; you just have to go through it.

Around this time, I walked into the office of my family doctor and poured my heart out. I fell to my knees and cried the most heartfelt cry. When asked what I was feeling, I told the doctor that I wanted to jump out of my skin, sit myself in a corner, and run as far away from myself as possible. At the time, that's exactly how I felt. I didn't even know who I was anymore. The only thing I knew was that I was a desperate soul living in a body that was fading fast.

Now I think to myself, *I made it!* Listen to me when I tell you that *only God can do that!* He moved me!

God moved me from the job that sparked my career. He moved me from the man who I truly love. He took things from me that I fought my whole life to hold on to. He took things from me that I didn't even know I had. God stood me up in the middle of the driest desert, and he peeled every layer of me away until I was bare. He answered my prayers according to His will, not mine.

If someone had told me then that I would come out of that storm and see beauty in it, I would have boldly called him or her a liar. Oh, but the beauty that I have found in this. It's more than I would have ever imagined! We serve a mighty God and He loves us so much. Yes, he moved me. Yes, it felt like the end. Yes, he pieced me back together. Yes, he has made a new creation of me. I have a new heart and it's softer than I ever remember it being. He's given me a new set of eyes so I can view life through a different lens.

The Bible says that in the end Job was blessed with far more than he was given in the beginning. Like Job, I've since been given so much more than I ever had previously. The book of Job reveals so much more than the heart of a faithful believer. For me, it's proof that Satan has access to God, and he answers to Him. Let that sink in. Angels were created by God; therefore, He has authority over them just as He does over all creation. This shows that Satan himself can only be in one place at a time, and he cannot read our minds or get into our thoughts. If he could, he surely would have known that Job wouldn't crack under the pressure. Job's story proves that faith in God is always justified, no matter how helpless we feel at times.

The Cure

— **Matthew 5:14-16**

You are the light of the world. A town built on a hill cannot be hidden. Neither do people light a lamp and put it under a bowl. Instead they put it on its stand, and it gives light to everyone in the house. In the same way, let your light shine before others, that they may see your good deeds and glorify your Father in heaven.

There have been times when I've wondered if certain events were God speaking to me or if they were just mere coincidences. Other encounters were so clear and undeniable. I've wondered why God would put something on my heart that made me so uncomfortable I could have crawled under a rock. He has such a sense of humor!

I've heard time and time again that you never know what's on the other side of your obedience.

Ezekiel 36:26-27 says, "I will give you a new heart and put a new spirit in you; I will remove from you your heart of stone and give you a heart of flesh. And I will put my Spirit in you and move you to follow my decrees." His Word never returns void. This new heart of mine hasn't been the most popular. Although I sometimes think I sound crazy, that doesn't stop me from being vocal about what God is doing in me and through me.

I've found my greatest obstacle thus far has been sharing the Good News with those who don't understand it. I think to myself, maybe it isn't their time yet. Most times, God quickly intervenes and whispers, *"That's why you're here, Christina."*

I'll never forget watching the interview of American television presenter Kathie Lee Gifford after the passing of her longtime friend, evangelist Billy Graham. She rejoiced on national television as she recounted holding her late husband's lifeless body when he passed and how she praised God because she knew her husband was finally home. Her late husband is in heaven and so is Billy Graham.

In response to anyone who asked why she was so outspoken about her faith, she said: "If you had the cure for cancer, would you keep it quiet, or would you hold it and keep it a secret? And I always say, I have the cure for the malignancy of the soul—and He has a name—and it's Jesus."

Advancing God's Kingdom

— Romans 1:16-17

For I am not ashamed of the gospel, because it is the power of God that brings salvation to everyone who believes: first to the Jew, then to the Gentile. For in the gospel the righteousness of God is revealed—a righteousness that is by faith from first to last, just as it is written: "The righteous will live by faith."

The heartfelt inspiration behind my God Books and the journey that lead to this book being written was a strong desire to leave something to my girls who mean so much to me. I want them both to know and feel God's love for them. While I will always write in the hopes of my girls discovering an abounding love for the Lord, I truly believe this is God's way of reaching others through me.

God calls us to be fishers of men. We catch them, and He cleans them!

The Gospel of Luke tells a story about Jesus providing a miraculous catch of fish. It's one of the stories in the Bible that pulls on my heartstrings. Simon, who would later be called Peter, was a fisherman by trade. On this afternoon, Jesus stood near the Lake of Gennesaret, also known as the Sea of Galilee. As the crowd grew larger to listen to

Him, He noticed two boats on the water's edge, one of which belonged to Peter.

Jesus climbed into the boat and asked Peter to take him out a little way from the shore, so He could teach from the boat and more people could hear and see Him. I picture Him using the boat like a stage.

When Jesus had finished speaking, He turned to Peter and said, "Put out into deep water, and let down the nets for a catch." Luke 5:5 says that Peter responded to Jesus by saying, "Master, we've worked hard all night and haven't caught anything. But because you say so, I will let down the nets."

If I had to guess, Peter was probably thinking that he had been out on the water all day, he was exhausted, and the last thing he wanted to do was teach a carpenter from Nazareth how to fish.

Known to have been impulsive and quick to act, Peter often did and said things without thinking. I like to teasingly refer to him as the Duh-sciple!

He didn't know it at the time, but his decision to step out in faith and do as Jesus asked would change the course of his life forever. As soon as the nets were let down into the water, the catch of fish was so large that the nets began to break. With the help of other fishermen, they were able to fill both boats so full of fish that they began to sink. In amazement, Peter fell to his knees before Jesus and tells Him, in essence, that he isn't worthy to be in the presence of someone so great and magnificent. To which Jesus looks down at Peter and says, "Don't be afraid; from now on you will fish for people." And, just like that, Peter left his life as he knew it and set out to follow Jesus.

This is what Jesus says to us too: *"Hey, Christina, do you remember that storm I carried you through? It was just a storm. What started as a test is now your testimony. Now you go and fish for people. You catch them; I'll clean them!*

The Chosen One

— **Mark 6:4**

A prophet is not without honor except in his own town, among his relatives and in his own home.

If someone were to ask me how to grow closer to God, I'd tell them to look no further than His Son and the stories about Him in the Bible. Learn about the people—the ordinary people—who shared in His ministry and who believed in Him. This is where I personally discovered the true character of God. I also found it revealed in the way Jesus loves people. He ate with sinners and healed the sick. He acknowledged the lepers and prostitutes. He was bold! Diving into the Bible at the period of time before Jesus was crucified, you can read about the many ways that He shook things up.

Learning about Jesus—what He did, how He acted, who He spent time with, and understanding His personality—will bring you closer to Him.

I've come to discover, though, that there's such an overall misconception about who Jesus really is, what kind of people he gravitated towards, and why—in today's world and back when Jesus lived. In order to better understand why there was a great cloud of doubt surrounding Jesus being the Messiah in His day, you must first understand the expectations that the people of Jesus' time had for their long-awaited Messiah.

Jewish people in that time longed to be delivered from the heavy hand of Roman paganism. They believed their Messiah would be a political leader of some sort who would overthrow Rome and restore Israel. They envisioned a mighty and strong king who would ride in on a big horse with sharp swords. But then along comes Jesus, the son of a carpenter from Nazareth, and He's riding what? *A donkey?!* Talk about a plot twist. HA!

They were so busy looking for the "Son of David," a conqueror who would restore an earthly political kingdom, that they missed Jesus! They overlooked the true Messiah because He didn't fit the description of what they thought He should look like. Jesus didn't ride in with swords; his weapons were peace, love, and acceptance. The religious leaders wanted someone who agreed with what they did.

Instead, they got Jesus, the one who called out their sin and labeled them as hypocrites. He stirred the pot. In their minds, they had worked hard to get to where they were, and they believed in what they believed. Who was *He* to call them fakes and phonies?

The Chosen One. That's who!

The Lesson of Humility

— Luke 18:10-14

Two men went up to the temple to pray, one a Pharisee and the other a tax collector. The Pharisee stood by himself and prayed: 'God, I thank you that I am not like other people—robbers, evildoers, adulterers—or even like this tax collector. I fast twice a week and give a tenth of all I get.' But the tax collector stood at a distance. He would not even look up to heaven, but beat his breast and said, 'God, have mercy on me, a sinner.' I tell you that this man, rather than the other, went home justified before God. For all those who exalt themselves will be humbled, and those who humble themselves will be exalted.

Jesus had a way of turning the tables on the religious leaders of His time. They despised Him for the way He spoke, and they often looked for reasons to arrest Him. Many of them also looked down on the common people and despised sinners without acknowledging themselves as sinners also.

The Pharisees in particular considered themselves righteous because they followed every rule they made up for themselves. They believed their traditions were as solid as God's Word and that if they kept all of their traditional rules, they wouldn't transgress the commandments themselves. So, they put all their time and energy into following these rules and restrictions as perfectly as possible. They were dedicated to appearing entirely pious on the outside.

But then right there in the middle of all their rules and sanctimonious self-righteousness was Jesus, eating with tax collectors, associating with prostitutes, and forgiving sins! *Who is this man who forgives sinners? Only God can forgive sins! If He really is God's Chosen One, He wouldn't be near such filth!* This is how they felt about Jesus.

There are many parables told by Jesus throughout the Gospels. In Luke 14:7-11 Jesus teaches about seeking honor. I've spent a lot of time pondering why I am so fascinated by this story, and I think I'm intrigued by how deftly Jesus handles his opponents.

The Pharisees and experts of the law often invited Jesus to dinners or gatherings in an effort to trap Him. They watched and waited for Him to do or say something that would justify arresting Him. But He always knew of their intentions and outwitted them—*always!* He never hesitated to warn them of their arrogance. This parable is a lesson on humility and, boy, is it a good one!

Jesus found himself on Pharisee turf, which happened often. As He approached, He noticed a large table with most of the seats already taken by other guests, all seats of honor that were close to where the host sat. One empty seat was left all the way down at the farthest end of the table, so Jesus took that seat and, as the dinner commenced, He grabbed everyone's attention.

I can almost picture Him reclining on the far end of the table as He raised His hand and said, "Ahem. Yes. You all the way over there. Hi. Can you hear me? I just wanted to let everyone know that this is the best seat, the seat of least importance. When someone invites you to a feast, always choose this seat! Do not take the best seat because there may be someone more distinguished than you at the table."

If I had to guess, there were probably several religious leaders mumbling under their breath as they sat in those seats of honor listening to Jesus as He spoke.

He didn't stop there; I love what He said next. He stated, "If there is someone more important than you, the host will ask you to give up your seat and you will do the walk of shame, dressed in humiliation. So, the next time you are invited, take the lowest seat, so that when your host comes, he will ask you to move to a better seat, and you will be honored in the presence of the other guests."

It's no surprise that we live in a world where many times the value of a person is determined by their social status. Being humble is often mistaken as looking down on ourselves. Rather, it's acknowledging our sinfulness and our human nature. It's putting ourselves in a position to serve others instead of serving ourselves.

Humility is not self-degradation; it's a realistic assessment of our own importance and a commitment to serve.

My Roots

— **Ephesians 5:21**

Submit yourself to one another out of reverence for Christ.

I've always loved sitting across the table from my grandma and listening to her stories. She's wise and quite the storyteller. I can only imagine what it must have been like to sit near Jesus and listen to Him teach. There's just something about a story, like the parables in the Bible, that soothes my soul.

I consider myself fortunate to have many memories of my grandparents on my mom's side, as well as my dad's, although the memories I have of my Gamzy and Pops are childhood memories because they both passed on many years ago.

My Pops made the best Donald Duck voice, and it never got old. Anytime I called home "sick" from school, he came to my rescue in his light blue Oldsmobile. Meanwhile, Gamzy loved to make peanut butter fudge. I can still see her sitting in her recliner with her rosary beads in her hand. Oh, the looks she gave us out of the side of her eyes if we continued to go in and out of the house while she was praying. My roots were planted on Clara Street.

I know how blessed I am to still have my mom's parents with us. My grandpa celebrated his 95th birthday earlier this year, and my grandma blew his birthday candles out for him. That's just how she rolls! They say opposites attract; no other statement could ever hold more truth when it comes to Marie and Sweet Tabor!

My grandpa is so humble. A kindhearted, genuine, soft-spoken man, he laughs at his own jokes (it's so cute). He's never met a stranger. And people find it hard to believe that he worked his entire life—well, past his 90th birthday at least. As I write this, he is six months away from his 96th birthday, and he still loves to go to "the dance," as he says, and "shake a leg."

He just renewed his driver's license earlier this year. It's funny to think that he was almost unable to renew due to his age. I'm not sure if he sweet-talked the lady at the local DMV or if they figured out that he could back up his standard transmission truck better than most men half his age, but when asked what he is going to do when his license expires in another four years, he chuckled and said, "Well, I guess I'm just going to have to renew it again."

There's an old saying: "Behind every great man is a great woman." Well, I prefer the other version: "Behind every great man is a woman rolling her eyes." That would be my grandma! Marie G. TAY-bor, as she pronounces it.

She has such a dry sense of humor, and we all love her for it. There's an ongoing joke in our family that I believe started with my younger brother. He tells my oldest daughter, Madison, "If you ever do something really bad, don't tell your sister and don't tell Maw Maw because they are going to tell everybody your business!" This is the *truth*!

There are so many ways that I love her, but above all I love that she doesn't hide from who she is. I genuinely admire that about her. She's bold and honest, a lot like Jesus.

My Uncle Noon, who always greets me by saying "Hiiii, Lucy" once said, "Lucy, when you've lived as long as they have, you've earned the right to say what you want." When she speaks, people listen. Mostly to see what kind of sarcastic remark will come out of her mouth, but also because she's a good speaker. If you ever find yourself needing an entertaining story, take a seat at her kitchen table. You will likely find a range of hand gestures as she speaks (I now know exactly where I get this from) and my grandpa, sitting with his cowboy hat on and shaking his head because she could have very well told you the same story three different times without even blinking an eye.

I'll never forget one Sunday when my girls and I visited, and it just so happened that my mom had just left after spending a few nights with them. As I was sitting at the kitchen table, my grandma stood near the sink with one hand on her hip and the other resting on the counter. She said, "Christina, let me tell you about your momma. She's *not* the woman she used to be."

Okay, so let's pause for a minute! If you can just imagine a 5'1" ball of fire rolling her eyes while saying this. She's so overly dramatic! My very measured response was, "What did she do now, Maw Maw?"

Grandma explained to me that she had asked my mom to make a roux for her to which my mom had replied that she'd do it when she was ready. Later that afternoon, I called my mom and told her that Maw Maw was mad at her. She immediately exclaimed, "She told you about that damn roux, didn't she?"

Well, it turns out that Marie G. TAY-bor wanted her roux cooked when she wanted her roux cooked, which just so happened to be in the wee hours of the morning. And when my mom told her that she would make it as soon as she was up and about, Maw Maw decided to take matters into her own hands. My mom recounted to me, "Girl, when I walked in that kitchen, she had roux flying everywhere!"

My brother always jokingly says, "When my grandma tells you to do something, you're going to do it, and you're going to like it!", which makes us all laugh.

She and my grandpa never had much, but they always had each other. They are rich in ways that truly matter.

The Upper Room

— **Psalm 147:3**

He heals the brokenhearted and binds up their wounds.

In March of 2015, my family suffered a devastating loss when my dad lost another brother. It was the third funeral he and my Uncle Jerry would plan or participate in for a sibling. There's a hurt that radiates in the depths of my chest as I go back in my mind to the week or two following my Uncle Artie's death.

He was more than just an uncle to my siblings and me. There were no aunts and uncles in the Andre' family, more like bonus moms and dads, only funnier and less "parenty," for lack of a better word. You know the common saying that it takes a village to raise kids—something I've since confirmed while raising my own children! Well, he was such a huge part of our village. My younger brother learned to catch frogs with a broken arm because of my Uncle Artie. Their bond was unexplainable.

It makes me laugh when I think back to a birthday party a few years before he passed. My brother had been in law enforcement for a few years by then. As we stood outside, Uncle Artie joked about the next time he would travel Highway 90 toward Lake Charles and would pass through New Iberia. He said (in his Artie voice), "Noona-Bug, what's the number on your police unit? Next time I'm passing through, I'm dialing 911 and I'm saying I need Unit 109. *Man downnn, man downnnnn.*" He always extended his words when he was being funny. Shortly after, he would usually laugh at himself and say, "Get you someeeeee!" It was a given—we were either laughing at Uncle Artie or laughing at Uncle Jerry as he did the alligator dance on the floor!

Like most of our family, Uncle Artie and my dad always got a kick out of imitating actors from certain movies, like *Life* starring Eddie Murphy and Martin Lawrence. One of their favorite parts of the movie is when Claude and Ray are sitting down on a bench and they make a pact with each other: no matter who passes away first out of the two of them, the other will "bust up" in the funeral singing "The Upper Room."

It wasn't until the moment everyone stood near the mausoleum as the burial was near completion that my dad broke the silence and explained that not too long before, he and my Uncle Artie had made the same pact as they watched the movie together one night. As my dad loudly counted to three, my heart smiled and every single person at the same moment loudly sang, "The upper rooooom."

As I write this, I can picture my Uncle Artie laughing and saying, "Tell 'em 'bout the gun line, boss!" To those who know and love him, you will read this and say that line at least once in your Artie voice!

When someone we love passes from this life unexpectedly, there are so many questions left unanswered. We hurt for ourselves, and that's okay. The hours turn into days, and the days start to run into each other. Grief is a lot like a big, wet blanket because it sticks to you and feels so unbearably heavy. My Aunt Barbara said once that, "Grief is a great equalizer; it brings us all to our knees, which is where my help was found."

My outlook on death is much different than it used to be. I used to think that God took Uncle Artie too soon, but I've come to realize that God doesn't take our loved ones—He receives them.

As believers, we should rejoice just as Kathie Lee Gifford rejoiced when Billy Graham passed on. I've found consolation in knowing that our loved ones in heaven don't miss us because heaven isn't bound by time. Instead, they expect us. I believe in my heart that when our soul leaves its earthly body and journeys to heaven, there will be familiar faces awaiting our arrival at those pearly gates. I believe those faces will be the people who shared special bonds with us here on Earth, as well as those we may not know as well but in some way had a positive influence on our lives.

I am not ready to leave this life, and I pray that God gives me enough work on this Earth to last a very long time, but I know without a shadow of a doubt that when my time is up, I will go to the place we all long to be. Only then will I truly be home in the peace that surpasses understanding. This is how He covers us.

Christina Andre'

The Purest Love of All

— Luke 15:4-7

Suppose one of you has a hundred sheep and loses one of them. Doesn't he leave the ninety-nine in the open country and go after the lost sheep until he finds it? And when he finds it, he joyfully puts it on his shoulders and goes home. Then he calls his friends and neighbors together and says, 'Rejoice with me; I have found my lost sheep.' I tell you that in the same way there will be more rejoicing in heaven over one sinner who repents than over ninety-nine righteous persons who do not need to repent.

I've often struggled to fully grasp the depth of God's love for us. I believe we all struggle with this at some point in our lives, and for me it's been a battle for most of my life. I've come to the conclusion that it's nearly impossible to understand this perfect, flawless love without understanding God's character. I can't count how many times my heart has fallen to my feet as I've listened to other believers voice their confusion about God's love for them. It's as if I can picture myself all those years before, confused and in disbelief that God Himself could love me so much that He gave His only Son as the atoning sacrifice for my sins.

I think the problem is that we place God on our playing field and often forget that he's God! He doesn't love like we love. He doesn't forgive like we "forgive." God is far greater than anything our human minds could ever comprehend. His love for us exceeds any amount of love that we could ever imagine giving or receiving. To be 100 percent transparent, I know for a fact that I could never love anyone enough to nail either of my children to a cross.

That is how much He loves us, and the beauty in His love is that all we have to do is receive it.

There's a worship song called "Reckless Love" that has always touched a part of my heart like no other. It took a while to piece together exactly what it meant to me, but every Sunday I hope to hear it during worship. There has been a great theological debate behind the term "reckless" being used to describe God's love. Would it be my word of choice? Probably not. But I think Cory Asbury's heart behind this song and its title is the exact heart that God intends for us.

There's a live recording of Asbury singing "Reckless Love," and I've listened to it on replay over and over, simply because of the way he stops and explains why he chose the term reckless to describe God's love. In the middle of the song, he changes the pace and delivers such a powerful punch:

"When I use the phrase, 'the reckless love of God,' I'm not saying that God Himself is reckless. I am, however, saying that the way He loves, is in many regards, quite so. What I mean is

this: He is utterly unconcerned with the consequences of His actions with regards to His own safety, comfort, and well being. His love isn't crafty or slick. It's not cunning or shrewd.

In fact, all things considered, it's quite childlike, and might I even suggest, sometimes downright ridiculous. His love bankrupted heaven for you and for me. His love doesn't consider Himself first. His love isn't selfish or self-serving. He doesn't wonder what He'll gain or lose by putting Himself on the line. He simply puts himself out there on the off chance that you and I might look and give him ourselves in return.

His love leaves the ninety-nine to find the one every time. To many practical adults, that's a foolish concept. 'But what if he loses the ninety-nine in search of the one?' What if? Finding that one lost sheep is, and will always be, supremely important.

His love isn't cautious. No, it's a love that sent His own Son to die a gruesome death on a cross. There's no 'Plan B' with the love of God. He gives His heart so completely, so preposterously, that if refused, most would consider it irreparably broken. Yet He gives Himself away again and again and again.

Make no mistake, our sins do pain His heart and seventy times seven is a lot of times to have your heart broken. Yet He opens up and allows us in every single time. His love saw you when you hated Him—when all logic said, 'They'll reject me,' He

said, 'I don't care what it costs me. I am laying My life on the line as long as I get their hearts.'

When I first set out to write this book, I didn't mention it to anyone. It took a long time to warm up to the idea that people might ask to read it one day, and I would have to be okay with that because that's what people do with books—they read them. It was very personal for me. In fact, it is still very personal, and the topics I discuss are not ones that everyone will agree with or understand. This, too, is something I had to accept—potentially being controversial.

Three or four months after I began writing, I emailed my dad a few pages to read. My dad has always been one of my greatest supporters, but admittingly, I was worried how he might respond. Would he agree or not agree? Would he think I was onto something or suggest that I should keep my day job?

Looking back, I realize how silly it was to be so anxious over how he might react. He is the kind of dad who would be equally proud whether I painted yellow polka dots on a rock or became the first female President of the United States of America. I received his reply a few hours later by email, and it caused me to stop and think for a while.

February 9, 2018 at 4:20pm

Sweetheart, I really enjoyed reading your thoughts on God. I find you struggled with many things we all struggle with as a human being and being Christian. The biggest thing I struggle with is (I'm not worthy of God's love and forgiveness). But

I've found everyone who is Christian thinks that way sometimes and even often. But God's Word is God's Word. Our faith tells us to believe, but we are human.

I love you so much. I'm so proud you call me daddy. I'm so blessed to have you in my life.

Love you sweetheart, Daddy

The irony of this is that I cannot think of anyone more worthy of God's love and forgiveness than my dad. His struggle is one that we all have or will struggle with at some point. But he's right. God's Word is God's Word, and our faith tells us to believe. God doesn't love us because of who we are. He loves us *despite* who we are.

Defining Moments

— **Proverbs 13:22**

A good person leaves an inheritance for their children's children, but a sinner's wealth is stored up for the righteous.

One of the hardest things about being a parent is knowing that I will not always be the most dominant influence in my daughters' lives. I have prayed and will continue to pray that God will reveal himself to my girls just as he has revealed Himself to me. The humor in this is that I still at times forget that God is in control. He reminded me of this one day as I asked my oldest daughter to read my manuscript and tell me what she thought about it.

At this point, my manuscript was written in cursive handwriting and confined to a five-subject spiral notebook. I had not yet considered using a laptop computer like most people would have. I was so excited when she agreed to read it, I could hardly contain myself. As I opened this ratty, old notebook to the first page and placed it in front of her on the counter, her face dropped.

Immediately, I thought it might have been too much, too soon for her. Maybe she wasn't ready? What if she hated it?

And then she looked at me with a confused facial expression and said, "Mom, I can't read this." I felt just as confused as she looked, if not more. She proceeded to tell me that no one had taught her or her classmates to read or write in cursive at school. If there was ever a time when a big, neon green sign could have hung above my head that read, "This is a defining moment in your life," this was it.

All those years I spent journaling in my God Books during church services, bible studies, and late-night cry sessions with the intention of leaving all those thoughts and revelations to my girls one day when I'm gone, and they couldn't even read my handwriting if they tried!

God wrecked my plan; He knew just what He was doing from the beginning. He took the compilation of God Books that was to be seen only by my girls, and He turned it into something bigger that would be shared with many people. That's what He does. He knew if I wrote those God Books in cursive that I would eventually either have to re-write that five-subject notebook in print, or I would just have to write a book to make sure that my girls could read all that I had written. I can't help but to laugh every time I tell this story. He has a habit of wrecking our plans in such a way that we can't help but be thankful in the end.

This book has been one of the hardest, yet most rewarding things that I have done so far in my life. There have been days when I felt so dry, I could not bear the thought of ever completing it. Other days, I am overflowing with God's Word and cannot get my thoughts on paper fast enough. I've taken a little something from both the good days and the bad. I am reminded that I am fully human, and my walk with God was never promised to be fairy dust and butterflies all of the time. Nevertheless, I find myself thankful that His Spirit dwells in me every day and not only on the good ones.

You're Invited!

— 1 Timothy 1:15-17

Here is a trustworthy saying that deserves full acceptance: Christ Jesus came into the world to save sinners—of whom I am the worst. But for that very reason I was shown mercy so that in me, the worst of sinners, Christ Jesus might display his immense patience as an example for those who would believe in him and receive eternal life. Now to the King eternal, immortal, invisible, the only God, be honor and glory for ever and ever. Amen.

What I have written in this book is the truth, the whole truth, and nothing but the truth as I know it. I believe these things not because of what someone has told me I should believe, but because of what God has revealed to me over time. If it was possible to shout to the world in every language known to man about the goodness that God has poured upon me, I would do just that. Instead, this book is my shout to the world—just ink and paper, along with unending hope and heartfelt prayers that my compilation of God Books will cause a stirring in your heart.

In the past, whenever I sat next to a Christian who, from the outside looking in, appeared to have the perfect life, their attempts to tell me how great our God is didn't awaken my heart and spirit. If anything, in those moments I passed judgement on those Christians. I hesitate to say that now because I have since learned that everyone has a story, and the outside appearance of a person rarely ever reflects what's on the inside.

Please don't discount my story the same way I previously judged those "perfect" Christians. My testimony is very different. I'm not perfect; instead, I have lived most of my life broken. God's still working on me, even now.

There's nothing pretty about this picture I am painting for you. Life has given me a pretty bad hand at times, and I have made an absolute mess of myself for far longer than I'd like to admit. But by the grace of God, this is not who I am anymore. The lyric is true: "If grace is an ocean, we're all sinking." Heaven knows I need all the grace I can get!

I often wonder how different my life would have been had I known of God's divine grace sooner. As mentioned before, I had always felt very distant from God and the idea of getting to know Him seemed far-fetched and downright difficult. I've come to realize that we often place difficulty where it doesn't belong.

Are you struggling just as I have? Are you unsure of where to start? Romans 10:9-11 says, "If you declare with your mouth that Jesus is Lord, and believe in your heart that God raised Him from the dead, you will be saved. For it is with your heart that you believe and are justified, and it is with your mouth that you profess your faith and are saved."

If this is you and you've come to a place where you're ready to accept God's grace and make Him the Lord of your life, I am so happy you are here! I hope you will accept my invitation to pray a prayer of salvation:

Dear Lord,

I believe you are the Son of God. I believe that on the cross, you bore my sin. I believe you took my guilt and my shame; you died for it. I believe that you faced hell for me so I wouldn't have to go. I believe you rose again on the third day to give me a place in Heaven, a purpose on earth, and a relationship with the Father. On this day, I confess and believe that I am born again. From this day forward, I turn away from sin. I will follow you all the days of my life. God is my Father, Jesus is my Savior, the Holy Spirit is my helper, and Heaven is now my home. In Jesus' name, Amen.

You will celebrate your spiritual birthday for a long time to come. What a true blessing! Welcome to the family!

www.ingramcontent.com/pod-product-compliance
Lightning Source LLC
Chambersburg PA
CBHW021413290426
44108CB00010B/507